Starting a *Young Adult* Group

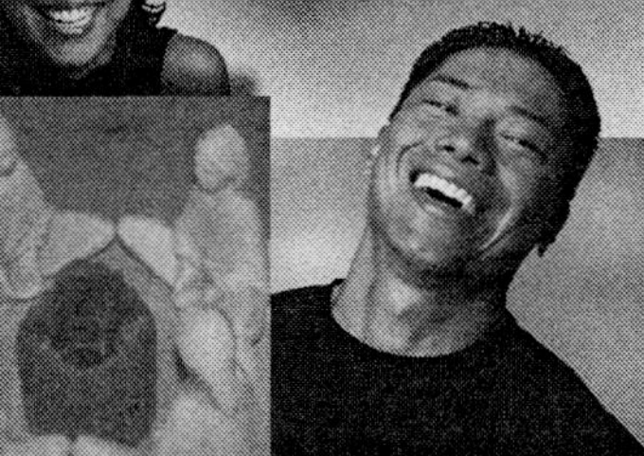

Kelly Phipps

Copyright © 2003
Herald Publishing House
Independence, Missouri
Printed in the United States of America

I dream of a place . . .

Where I can be myself, speak my mind, and not be ashamed to change when I am challenged;

Where I can mourn, celebrate, question, and learn;

Where honesty is expected and physical appearance is insignificant;

Where I feel God's concern for me through the actions of others;

Where the scriptures are not just read but applied to every aspect of my life today;

Where I can get help to become the person I want to be;

Where belief leads to action.

—young adult

Mission Statement

Community of Christ

We proclaim Jesus Christ and promote communities of joy, hope, love, and peace.

Acknowledgments

Many of the ideas in this book are not from the author. They are lessons learned from the young adult ministers who have failed at efforts that should have worked, been blessed with success in efforts that seemed doomed, and marveled when God created such amazing experiences from such humble contributions. It is from these experiences that this book comes.

Special thanks to those who contributed ideas:

Greg Ardito	Margo Frizzell
Andrew Bolton	Sandee Gamet
Monica Bradford	Jane Gardner
Steve Bradford	Carrie Garwood
Anthony Chvala-Smith	Jim Hannah
Charmaine Chvala-Smith	Jessica Hope
Tim Dodds	Bob Kyser
Rob Dowell	Diane McNeil
Todd Elkins	Jill Phipps

CONTENTS

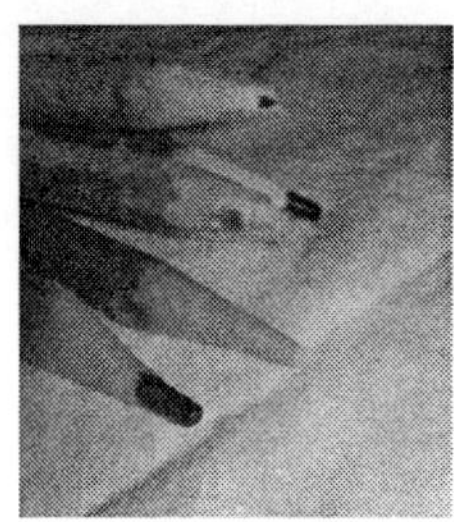

Overview of Process

Form a team.

Define your purpose.

Make a commitment.

Schedule your first meeting.

Invite others.

Welcome young adults.

Evaluate how you are doing.

Look for resources to grow.

Introduction

If you are reading this book, you have probably been asked to be a young adult leader, or perhaps you are feeling called to volunteer. Chances are, you are wondering where to start. This book was written for you. Each section was written in response to the question, "What should a young adult know before starting a young adult group?"

The advice found here is no substitute for a loving, experienced mentor. If you are a young adult, make sure that you find someone to help you grow in your leadership. If you are not a young adult any longer, use this information to help you become a mentor to a young adult with leadership potential. The best young adult ministry comes from young adults, supported by an experienced mentor who listens.

The structure of this book is based on a model that has been used by the church for generations to help small groups create a community where life and faith meet. This model proposes that a healthy group will engage in each of these four activities regularly:

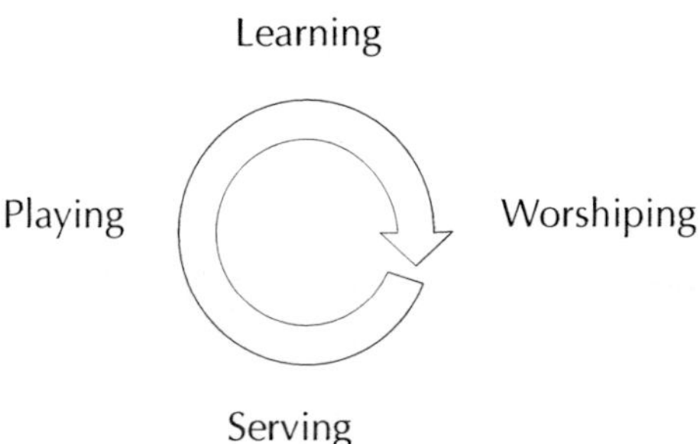

No two young adult groups will be the same, because no two young adults are the same. As a result, there is no set formula for creating a healthy young adult group, and not all of the advice in this book will apply to your situation. These suggestions are offered as our best effort at helping those who feel called to serve God in ministry with other young adults. May the joy and pain of growing together as followers of Christ bless you as it has us.

Key Points
- **The best young adult ministry comes from young adults, supported by an experienced mentor who listens.**
- **A healthy young adult group learns, plays, worships, and serves together.**

CHAPTER 1

Why?

Why Start a Small Group?

Young adults are exploring their faith. They are sorting through what they were taught, what they heard from their parents, what they have experienced, and what they are doubting, trying to form a collection of beliefs they can claim as their own. They are also looking for a place they can call their own, a place where they find relationships that support and challenge them, a place where they are accepted and feel at home. This book is intended to help young adults combine those two searches by intentionally forming small groups where young adults can explore their faith together.

Forming a small group for young adults is hard work. If your congregation is already small, you may be asking what is the point of forming an even smaller group. The answer is that Christianity is practiced in community. Developing Christian disciples requires a loving, trusting environment where both new Christians and those raised in the faith can experiment, explore, and discover what it means to be servants of God. While congregations exist to do just that, sometimes young adults need a safe place where they can be supported in their search by others in the same life stage. Young adult groups are one way of providing that safe place for all "seekers" to find the beginning nucleus of their faith.

Key Point
* **A young adult group exists to grow disciples of Christ.**

What Is a Disciple?

Working to develop disciples requires that we have some image in our minds of what that term means. While there is no universal definition of what it means to be a disciple, the "path of the disciple" referred to in Doctrine and Covenants 161:3d is an attempt to describe what it means to be a follower of Jesus. The elements of that path have been described as community, reconciliation, sharing, learning, spirituality, and justice.[*] These descriptions give us some clues about what a growing disciple might look like.

[*]W. Grant McMurray, "A Transforming Faith: A Call to Discipleship," *Saints Herald* 147 (June 2000): 183–191.

Below are several examples of how the elements of this path might be expressed in the life of a young adult. Obviously, each of us falls short of the example given by Jesus, and so this list will always have room for growth. Additional space is provided for you to add descriptions you think are central to being a disciple.

Community

A disciple is someone who . . .

- welcomes the stranger.
- cannot help but share with others the freedom they have found.
- lives their commitment to God in a community of believers that supports and helps them grow.
- ____
- ____

Reconciliation

A disciple is someone who . . .

- leaves destructive lifestyle choices behind and begins again with God's forgiveness.
- extends that same forgiveness to others.
- seeks ways to affirm the divine image they see reflected in each person, despite perceived differences.
- is becoming increasingly skilled in the processes of reconciliation and diligently practices these in all their relationships.
- ____
- ____

Sharing

A disciple is someone who . . .

- recognizes their stewardship in creation and generously shares from the wealth they manage for God.
- uses their time, money, and talents to assist the poor, the oppressed, and the needy.
- identifies the gifts that God has given them and uses them to serve God.
- happily shares with others their personal experience with God.
- ____
- ____

Learning

A disciple is someone who . . .

- is encountering the scriptures, "by study and faith."
- is constantly seeking to expand their knowledge, while recognizing that our understanding will always be limited.
- recognizes that not everyone will hold the same perspectives or values, and sees other's perspective as a source to learn from.
- ________________________________
- ________________________________

Spirituality

A disciple is someone who . . .

- recognizes the importance of affirming God in every aspect of their life.
- prays and meditates regularly.
- responds to life with gratitude to God.
- is hopeful about the future and God's ability to bring joy out of any suffering.
- ________________________________
- ________________________________

Justice

A disciple is someone who . . .

- looks to Jesus as an example of how God created humans to live.
- values the equal worth of all people.
- makes decisions not by the values of their culture but by the values demonstrated by Jesus.
- finds their identity not in possessions or in power, but in being a servant minister.
- ________________________________
- ________________________________

All of us, including young adults, are growing in our discipleship. An effective young adult group will create a challenging, accepting environment for those just beginning their journey as disciples, while engaging those further along as ministers to model Christian discipleship.

CHAPTER 2

Planning

Forming a Team

Many young adults say of their congregation, "I would plan something for other young adults, but I am the only one." The most effective young adult groups started with one or two individuals who had a vision, but they did not do it alone. Finding at least one other person inspired with the same vision and willing to work with you is an important first step. A leadership team, even if it is only two of you, will help you see concerns you would have missed and will also be an important support for you when the inevitable struggles come along. Groups that appeal to diverse people are led by diverse leaders.

Skills to have represented in the team
someone who looks out for the underrepresented
   (the lonely, the shy, the poor)
someone with good organizational and communication skills
someone who is sensitive to the feelings of others
someone who is enthusiastic about communicating with others

Attitudes for all team members to foster
willingness to listen to the viewpoints of others
ability to speak one's opinion honestly without attacking others
willingness to change one's opinion
willingness to pray together, and seek God's guidance for the group

Finding others willing to be leaders can be a struggle, especially if there aren't many young adults active in your area. For you, this may be less like forming a team and more like spreading the vision. Remember to look beyond the young adults already active in the congregation. Try looking in old camp logs and church school rosters to find names of young adults who might still be in the area. Those who don't attend Sunday morning church may be looking for a new way to feel connected and involved in a community of believers. Look to friends outside church who are searching for a spiritual community. Even if they are not willing to be leaders, they may be interested in being involved once the group is started.

Key Points
- **This can't be done alone.**
- **Having leaders with different strengths is important.**
- **Some of the greatest commitment may come from those not active in church right now.**

Mentors

MENTORS

Starting a young adult group may be your first experience in the role of "minister." That is why it is critical that you have an experienced minister to serve as your mentor. While young adult groups should be led by young adults, every leader can benefit from the support of a caring, sensitive mentor. Having a congregational leader initially serve as one of the leadership team can provide stability and depth to a starting group. Even if they only assist in the initial stages of planning, an experienced minister can help you navigate obstacles that might otherwise end the group before it starts.

Choosing the right person to be your mentor is critical. You should look for someone whose ministry is respected and well received by young adults. Look for that person who young adults seek out and maintain contact with, even when the young adults are not actively attending church. It is crucial that the mentor you choose is someone who is willing to listen more than they talk to the young adults, and that they are willing to help grow leaders to take their place.

Key Point
- **Find a mentor.**

Clarifying the Goal

GOALS

It is easy to begin the planning stage by focusing first on the details of how the group should function. But before you get too specific, take some time as a leadership team to consider why you are working together. Talk together about the following:

What is missing in our individual lives?

Why do we think this group should exist?

Are we responding to God's call, or is something else motivating us?

Once you feel that you understand why you are working together, talk together about what goal you are working toward. It is critical that your leadership team clearly understands a common goal. This can be a time-consuming process, and in the midst of the struggle some people can feel like it would be easier to do nothing. That is natural. The goals you develop at this stage do not have to be final and should be reviewed over time. However, the work you put into defining goals will greatly reduce tensions that can develop later when differing goals begin to surface.

Here are some key questions for your leadership team to answer before the first meeting of your group is ever scheduled:

>What types of young adults do we feel called to reach out to?

>What feeling do we want our gatherings to have?

>If someone were to attend this group for six months, how do we hope they would describe it to a friend?

Carl George, an author on small group dynamics, suggests that there are three reasons for a small group to exist:

1. Provide nurturing relationships.
2. Invite others to Christ.
3. Grow new leaders so more groups can be formed.[*]

He suggests that most small groups accomplish the first objective, but the second and third require real effort and planning. If your group is going to be anything more than a social network, you will need to begin setting those expectations from the start.

Key Points
- **Talk together about why you are forming the group.**
- **Future conflicts can be avoided if common goals are formed at the beginning.**

*Carl F. George, *Nine Keys to Effective Small Group Leadership* (Mansfield, Pennsylvania: Kingdom Publishing, 1997), 1.

Making a Commitment

COMMIT

No one wants to commit to a responsibility that has no end in sight, especially if they are unsure what that responsibility will involve. However, groups do not succeed without committed leaders. As a leadership team, decide how long you are willing to commit to this new group. A year-long commitment to a program that is not working doesn't help anyone. Start with a commitment that feels right for you, and schedule periodic meetings to evaluate how things are going.

Remember that forming a strong small group takes time, and it may not happen by the time your first evaluation meeting comes. Your commitment is not to reach all your goals by that date but to offer your best for that time, and then reevaluate how to proceed from there. You can always agree together to continue longer or adapt to a new format in response to what you have learned in your experience. Leaders who feel trapped are usually not effective leaders.

A trusting community cannot be built if members are always unsure if there will be another meeting. Part of the commitment you make as a leader is to make sure the opportunity is there for other young adults to attend. This may mean that sometimes you are the only one who attends. Talk about this as a leadership team, and discuss how you will handle making sure meetings are held regularly. The commitments you make need not be permanent, but they do need to be kept.

Key Points

- **Commit to a trial length for the group, and schedule evaluation meetings.**
- **Make sure scheduled meetings happen.**

Deciding When and Where to Meet

SCHEDULE

Deciding when and where to meet can be a frustrating task. Even deciding how often to meet can become a long discussion. However, the frequency and location of your meetings will have a significant impact on what your group becomes. In general, the more frequent your gatherings, the more quickly and deeply your community will form. Below are a number of different models chosen by other young adult groups that have formed.

Sample Models of Young Adult Ministry

- weekly gathering at a church
- Sunday morning young adult class
- weekly scripture study in homes
- twice monthly meetings at a central location
- monthly service projects
- quarterly retreats
- a combination of any of these

As you try to decide what will work best for you, here are some thoughts to consider:

- Choose a location that is best suited to the type of group you want to create. For some, a church setting is just what they are looking for. For others, a public place or a home may be the best environment for the group they are forming.

- The frequency of your meetings is a product of various factors, such as how close together your target group lives, what life stage the young adults are in, and how much time the leaders have to commit. Again, choose what works best for your group, but be aware that the less frequent your gatherings, the more work your publicity will be. Consistent times and locations, such as weekly, require little in the way of reminder phone calls and postcards, while monthly gatherings require monthly reminders, at a minimum. If weekly gatherings are a possibility for your group, they also permit people to decide spontaneously to attend. Most people may not attend every week, but they always know there will be a gathering when they can attend.

- You will probably never find a time that everyone can meet, so try your best to choose a time that will permit the most people to attend. Remember to seek out feedback from those outside the leadership team when making this decision.

Key Point
- **The less frequently you meet, the more frequently you need to publicize.**

Inviting

The most persuasive invitation for most young adults is a personal invitation from a friend. In addition, many young adults need to hear about an activity three or four times, in three or four different ways before they decide to attend. This means you can't just rely on an announcement in the church bulletin to get the word out. You may need to make phone calls, send postcards, e-mails, and reminder notes.

Start by making a list of all the young adults you can think of who might be interested in being a part of this group. Get out old camp logs and track down young adults you haven't seen in years. Check with parents and grandparents of young adults in the congregation to see who they know might be interested. Think about your friends at school or work. Ask those who attend the first meeting to invite their friends. Think of your efforts not as announcing an activity but personally inviting other young adults to be a part of something that matters. In all your contacts, remember that your goal is not attendance but ministry. Not everyone will respond, or even appreciate the invitation, but your contact will show them that others care about them, even if they choose not to be a part.

For the cost of postcards or long distance phone calls, your congregation or jurisdiction may have a budget to assist in the cost. Be sure to check with your pastor or jurisdictional leader before relying on those funds. They may also be able to run a list of young adults on the congregational or jurisdictional rolls. You may find it helpful to identify a member responsible for maintaining a mailing list of members and invitees. It is important than an effort is made to invite even the young adults you don't know, to avoid forming what might be viewed from the outside as a clique, where only certain people are welcome.

Key Points
- **Personal invitations are best.**
- **It is important to invite young adults beyond your circle of friends, especially if they are not currently active in church.**

CHAPTER 3

Starting

Welcoming and Involving

The first few minutes of your first meeting, or any meeting where a new person is visiting, are crucial. Most people feel a little awkward when they are new to a group. How the young adults feel about the group will be shaped by their experiences in those first few moments, and it may determine whether they will come back. As a leadership team, talk about what feeling you want young adults to have when they first arrive, and how you can structure the physical environment, program, and responsibilities to evoke that feeling.

Ideally, when a new person attends they should learn something about each member of the group, without feeling singled out themselves. Below are some ideas for welcoming and involving new members.

- Have someone assigned to greet young adults at the door.
- Involve young adults in some activity as soon as they arrive, such as cooking a meal, preparing snacks, or arranging the room.
- Make sure that everyone knows one another's name, and be sure to reintroduce yourselves the first couple of times someone visits. As your group grows, you may want to consider nametags for everyone, especially if you have visitors often.
- Begin your meetings with a nonthreatening activity that involves everyone, such as sharing a high or low point from the last week.
- Be sure to explain any traditions or recurring activities if there are new people present.
- If asking anyone to participate, such as offering a prayer, be sure to ask in private so that they are not embarrassed to decline.

Money

Young adults will give money to what is important to them. However, as a general rule, young adults in their twenties don't have much money to give. For this reason, try to avoid scheduling activities that cost or that might exclude those who are low on funds. When activities that cost are scheduled, try to give an opportunity for everyone to contribute as much as they are able. Even if the congregation or an individual benefactor is willing to pay for all or part of the cost of an activity, it can create a feeling of dependence and can actually make a young adult less likely to attend if they feel they are a financial burden on others. Ultimately, the most meaningful activities your group can do together cost nothing, and the creative search for inexpensive ways to be together may be the greatest team-building activity you find.

Invariably, some part of your time together will cost money. If your group wants to have a regular meal together or other activity that involves cost, you can put out a plate for a minimal suggested donation of a dollar or two. While this may not fully cover the cost of the meal, it gives the young adults a chance to contribute as much as they are able, without feeling uneasy about "freeloading." The remaining cost could be covered by the congregation, jurisdiction, or a donor. Whenever you collect money, be sure that everyone knows what the money is to be used for, and make sure that the group has input in those decisions.

Often groups are offered "start-up" money, or a donor offers to help the group with costs for a while. This show of support is certainly good news and can be a sign that others have high hopes for the success of the group. However, there are some side effects to accepting large amounts of money that you should keep in mind. First, remember that activities can easily grow into whatever budget they are given. If the money will not continue to be available, be careful not to become accustomed to a level of spending your group cannot support on its own. Second, money from outside the group can sometimes come with expectations. While the expectations of most donors are usually in line with the goals of the group, sometimes the two will differ. Future conflict can be avoided if the group's mission is clarified and widely known, members are involved in making financial decisions, and budgets are kept modest.

Key Points
- **Try to avoid activities that cost money.**
- **Provide a chance for young adults to contribute as much as they can to activities that do cost money, and be clear what the money is being collected for.**
- **Keep budgets modest.**

Food

FOOD

It is hard to adequately emphasize the importance of food at a young adult activity. Food brings people together, keeps people busy, and saves them from having to approach someone they do not know. Just like many families gather in the kitchen, most young adults gather where the food is. This does not mean that you need to offer a full meal, or that the food needs to be expensive, but having food available can help create an atmosphere of inclusion.

Key Point
- **Food helps.**

Patience, Prayer, and Realistic Expectations

PRAYER

The time leading up to your first few meetings will be very exciting as you wait to see who will show up. However, the truth is that most young adult groups start small, and many remain small. While optimism is important, disappointment following unrealistic expectations can overshadow an otherwise healthy start.

If you feel strongly that your group must start big, ask yourself why you feel that way. If you are especially concerned about whether the group will "succeed" or "fail," you may be overly attached to your image of what the group should look like. While it is easy to be guided by a desire to avoid looking foolish or to be seen by others as a successful minister, it is ultimately God's desires for the group that matter the most. As a servant minister, you must be willing to accept the outcome when you have offered your best efforts. The results are often surprises that could never have been anticipated.

It is critical for the leaders to pray together as preparations are made for the first meeting. Prayer reinforces that starting a young adult group is a practice of servant ministry, not salesmanship. Prayer also helps leaders avoid the temptation to form the group to meet only their own personal needs. Through prayer, you can begin to sense the direction God is calling the group to go.

For some groups, only the leaders showed up at the first meeting. This is obviously discouraging, but should not be the sole reason for stopping your efforts. Young adults are notorious for waiting to see if something will last before getting involved. It may take several months of consistent offerings before others are convinced this is not just another short-lived attempt to reach young adults. Regardless of what attendance looks like at those first few meetings, remember that young adult groups are about ministry, not attendance.

Key Points
- **Starting small is natural.**
- **The goal is ministry, not attendance.**

Continuing

Communicating with the Congregation

It is important for young adults to have a place where they can explore their faith together and form relationships with others their age. However, it is also critical that young adults have relationships with those outside their age range. Maintaining a connection with the larger congregation can provide those relationships and guard against isolationism.

Maintaining that connection with a congregation can be work. Since decisions are made within the group, be sure that someone has the responsibility of sharing periodically with the pastor how things are going. A small investment of time in keeping the congregation informed will go a long way toward opening doors for ministry and coordination. A healthy young adult group is a ministry of the congregation, not a replacement for the congregation.

Consider some of the following ways to maintain connection with the congregation:

- Invite the pastor to join you for a particular activity.
- Post a photo of your group in the church so that members can see who is attending and feel involved.
- Ask a mentor from the congregation who understands and relates well with young adults to attend periodically or assist in a leadership role.
- Periodically have the small group plan or participate in a Sunday morning worship service.
- Occasionally invite a member of the congregation to teach a class on something in which they are skilled.

Young adult groups that are not connected with a congregation in some way can struggle with questions of direction. Without a tie to a larger community, a group can struggle with understanding what the ultimate goal of their group is. Are they planting a church? Is it an exclusive church? What happens when members are no longer young adults? Small groups that are connected with a congregation struggle less with those questions, since many of them are answered by the existence of the congregation.

Key Points
- Look for ways to keep the congregation involved and informed.
- A healthy young adult group is a ministry of the congregation, not a replacement for the congregation.

Reviewing the Goals

When your group has been meeting for a while, it is important to review the goals you originally set. As a team, ask the following questions:

- Are we doing what we set out to do?
- Does the group have the feeling we originally intended? If not, why not?
- What traditions have we established that we want to continue?
- What traditions are not working and need to be replaced or abandoned?
- How can we improve what we are doing?
- What new opportunities have opened that we did not originally envision?
- How have we seen God at work in our group?
- Who needs to be involved in the leadership team, and how do we prepare them to assume leadership?
- Are we willing to continue? for how long?
- When should we meet again to evaluate?

Evaluating is more than seeing whether you are accomplishing your goals. No matter how much you have prepared, you will learn a lot in your first few months. Be sure to give yourself the flexibility to change direction and modify goals as you learn.

Key Point
- Schedule a time to review the goals.

Expanding Leadership

EXPAND

Leadership is a critical issue to be examined both in forming the group and in expanding the group. In most cases, if the group is going to survive beyond the first year, the leadership team will need to expand. No one can carry all the responsibility indefinitely, and leaders who don't have help can burn out quickly. As the group grows, members will need to clarify what functions need leadership and form a structure that best suits the membership and goals. But most importantly, if the group is going to grow, members need to begin to take ownership. It is important that you begin early to think about who your core group is and how to involve them in ways that use their gifts.

Leadership decisions are often made by holding a group meeting and asking who wants to be in charge. This approach is seldom effective at increasing the leadership base or involving the right people in the right way. In a group setting, individuals can sometimes be shy about saying what they think they are good at or afraid of being overwhelmed with responsibility. If you intend to proceed in this way, make sure that people have ample notice and opportunity to prepare for the planning meeting.

As an alternative, consider asking people what they are feeling called to share with the group, rather than asking who wants to accept a particular leadership position. When people are serving in roles they are excited about, both the group and the individual will grow. Also, most people are appreciative of hearing privately that others recognize their gifts. Consider approaching young adults before the planning meeting and letting them know you think they are good at something. These steps will help assure that your leadership team is made up of both willing and capable leaders.

Another aspect of expanding leadership is helping young adults who may have gifts but little or no experience. This means that the group will need to be patient and encourage new leaders as they learn. Consider assigning mentors either from inside or outside the group when new leaders begin their assigned roles. Helping individuals grow in leadership may be the most important thing your group does.

Ownership of the group can sometimes become an issue when leadership questions arise. As much as you try to respond as servants, it is easy for the leadership team to be perceived from the outside as "in charge," and thus the owners of the group. Try to instill in the group from the beginning the belief that the group belongs to God. Likewise, try to act in your leadership team in ways that respect God's call for the group, even if it may not seem like the direction you would choose.

Key Points

- **Make a point to expand your leadership team in the first year.**
- **Helping develop leaders may be the most important thing your group can do.**
- **New leaders may have gifts but no experience.**

Multiplying

MULTIPLYING

It is possible that your small group may get big. When the group gets so large that it is impossible to know one another well, the group needs to decide how it will respond. A couple of options are to change format from a small group to a large group or to multiply into several small groups. It may be possible to continue meeting in a large group for some activities, but to rely on multiple small groups to maintain the personal connections that a smaller group provides. Regardless of the direction you choose, be sure to discuss it thoroughly with a minister experienced in small group dynamics, since there are many factors to consider.

If your group reaches this point but ignores it, the decisions will be made for you. A group that grows too big to maintain relationships will begin to lose members. Reaching this point of crossroads may produce a sense of loss for some of your group, and this is natural. The group they have worked so hard to build now has to change. Try to remember that your group was created as a place where the gospel could be shared in people's lives. Having more communities where that can happen is a success, not a problem, in spite of the short-term feeling of loss. The blessing of community is never static.

Key Point

- **Small groups should be small enough to allow everyone to know each member well.**

Moving On

Nothing is permanent in young adult ministry. Because young adult ministry is about ministering with people in transition, your group will always be changing. Even though most people know that, it is still hard to see all you worked to create become only a memory.

A successful young adult ministry group is always changing, responding to the needs that exist today. While sometimes that means there will be a group meeting in the same location for many years, sometimes it also means that groups that were once thriving will stop meeting. Effective ministry is not measured by longevity but by the influence it has in people's lives. Even a ministry that continues will have to let go of the past and adapt to the present.

In addition to ending groups, each person will someday reach the end of their time as young adults. The best way to make that transition gracefully is to serve as a mentor to young adults younger than yourself. Help them create a group responsive to their needs. However, your group may decide to continue meeting beyond your young adult years. If you do, try to call yourselves something other than "young adult," so that those who follow you will still be able to create a group for themselves.

Key Points
- **Effective ministry is not measured by longevity but by influence.**
- **When you are no longer a young adult, become a mentor.**

CHAPTER 5

Struggles

Most young adult groups will experience at least some of the following struggles in their first year. While there are no easy answers, knowing the problem may arise can help you plan ahead.

What Ages Are Young Adults?

No matter how hard you try to avoid it, the question of what age we mean when we say "young adult" will come up eventually. Some groups have found it helpful to impose a clear age limit, while other groups have found that a rigid approach to age excludes and hurts the people they want to welcome. Ultimately, you will need to make a decision on how your group will approach the issue. As you consider your approach, here are a few things to remember:

- Not all people in their twenties or thirties are the same. Most of what churches offer to young adults is based not on their age, but on their life stage.
- Ask yourself whether a nineteen year old would feel comfortable in your group. It is okay to have multiple groups supporting people in their particular life stages. But a group calling itself a "young adult" group should be a place where those transitioning out of senior high will feel welcome. If they are not welcomed among the young adults, there may be no other place for them.
- Even clear definitions will eventually become unclear as members of your group age.

Married, Single, and Parents

Young adults are in a variety of life stages. Often that life stage has more to do with how a young adult sees the world and interacts with others than their age does. There are no standard answers to the question of whether a young adult group should be for singles, married couples, or parents, just as there is no ideal life stage. Ask yourself who you are feeling called to reach out to and why. Make a real effort to be inclusive, and work to be flexible and accepting of those in a different life stage.

Low Attendance

In spite of all your grand ideas, young adult groups most often start small. In fact, many young adult activities have only two or three people attend the first few activities. While this is not true of all groups, it should not discourage you if it happens in your group. Sometimes young adults need to wait to see if something is going to last before they commit to it. For this reason, try to avoid canceling a scheduled activity, except in extreme circumstances. Canceling just contributes to the tendency to remain tentative.

It is easy to slip into the belief that if not enough people attend, the group isn't worth the effort. Remember that small groups are small for a reason. They are small to allow people to really know one another, and explore together in a way that large groups don't permit. Rather than feeling badly because more people aren't coming, plan activities that make the most out of your group's size.

Spiritual Versus Social

It is common for young adult leaders to plan on starting with social activities and then moving gradually toward more spiritual activities. This seems like a natural way to start, since social activities are fun and tend to attract people, and spiritual activities can sometimes be awkward with strangers. However, before you start in this direction, here is another perspective to consider.

Experience suggests that it is extremely difficult to change the focus of a group once it has been formed. The reason is easy to see: people join a social group because they want a social group. It shouldn't be a surprise if they resist an effort to change the focus of the group they chose. It can be risky to start a social group with the hidden motive of turning it into a spiritual group in the future.

This is not to say that all young adult groups need to be exclusively spiritual or exclusively social. Authentic community will always blend the two. Try to find ways to help people connect socially in spiritual ways. There are enough organizations offering purely social activities, and the church doesn't need to compete with them. There aren't nearly as many places offering a chance to connect with others on a spiritual level. That is what church is about and should be the starting point for your planning.

There are lots of ways to incorporate the spiritual into social activities. Try to establish from the start a tradition of caring for one another and holding each other up in prayer, even at supposedly "social" activities. Here are some examples of traditions you might choose or adapt to the needs of your group:

- Start every gathering by having each person share a good thing or a bad thing from their day or week, then have someone offer a prayer over what has been shared.
- End each gathering with a circle prayer, giving everyone a chance to say a sentence of prayer or participate silently.
- Play games that encourage sharing and building relationships, rather than highly competitive or adversarial games.
- Have a "show and tell" time regularly, and have at least one member of your group prepare to share briefly something that is spiritually meaningful to them.
- Include in each session a short devotional or reflective scripture reading.
- Schedule a regular time of silence together to pray and meditate.

Despite your planning, sometimes groups will form as primarily social, because the participants are not yet comfortable being spiritual together. In those cases, you may need to be patient, continually holding up something more, until the group decides for themselves that they want something more than games and snacks.

Inward Focus

Most of what has been discussed so far has been about working to form a close community. However, once you have been blessed with that closeness, it can be difficult for new people to feel they belong. This is natural, but it can easily lead to the decline and eventual end of the group. The very nature of the good news of the gospel is that it must be shared. When you stop sharing it, it ceases to be good news. Here are some suggestions for dealing with the tendency toward inward focus:

- Involve all the members of your group in the process of seeking out new members from the start. If everyone sees themselves as a recruiter for the group, they are more likely to make sure visitors are welcome.
- Pay attention to how first-time visitors and repeat visitors are treated. Do they seem to be welcomed into the group? Is there a sub-group that is not accessible to newcomers? Are traditional activities explained to newcomers?
- Have an open process for how members become members. For example, if you have a list of members of the group, or certain planning committees, be clear about how newcomers can be added to that list or committee.

- Consider having a "visitor's" activity planned specifically for people to bring a first-time guest. Guests should be welcome any time, but visitors might be more comfortable if they knew they wouldn't be the only new person, and members might be more likely to invite a friend if they knew the activity was planned with visitors in mind.

- Watch for common characteristics that some members of your group might share that would make others feel excluded. If your group begins to attract only people of one type, ask yourselves how you can attract and welcome a more diverse group.

- Periodically ask the group members how they feel they are doing at maintaining an outward focus. Ultimately, welcoming new members is the responsibility of the entire group, not just the leaders.

Seekers and Believers

Members of your group may range from those absolutely sure of their beliefs to those who have never been in church or thought about what they believe. Many times those who are not sure of their faith, or who have never been exposed to questions of faith, can feel uncomfortable being with people who seem so sure of what they believe. In truth, most young adults are "seekers" in the sense that they are in the process of defining their own faith. Having a seeker in your group can be a real gift. There are many ideas and terms we take for granted in church life. It can be good for a group of believers to be pressed to describe what they believe and why to someone who is new to the faith. In the process, everyone grows.

Try to make sure that your group is welcoming to those who have little or no definition to their belief. Here are some suggestions on how to be welcoming of those just beginning to explore their faith.

- Avoid using terms or phrases that would not make sense to someone unfamiliar with church jargon. When it is used, be sure to explain it.

- When discussing issues of theology, ask yourself if a different opinion would be welcome.

- Use the questions of a seeker to help other members of the group define their faith. Avoid singling out the seeker.

- Recognize that no one's faith remains static. Respect the right of each person to grow in their understandings and change their opinion.

- If a seeker is looking for more information about church beliefs or teachings than you feel you can answer, ask congregational leaders for assistance. Also, *Seekers and Disciples* is a short resource designed to introduce the Community of Christ to seekers. It is available from Herald House.

Looking Good

Everyone wants people to think they are a good person. Most of us want others to see us as successful, intelligent, and attractive. But this is only part of who we really are. We have all failed at some time in our lives. That is part of what it means to be human. We have bad days and even bad years. We make bad choices, sometimes daily. We fail to live up to our potential. In order for your group to help grow authentic disciples, it is critical that the group become a safe place to share about failures and brokenness, regardless of whether they are past or present.

The good news that Christians preach and teach and sing is that we do not have to prove ourselves to God. God loves us not because of what we do, but because we are God's children. The amazing good news for all of us is that God can transform our failings into opportunities for ministry to others, all of whom are broken and loved just as we are. But, before our brokenness can be transformed into God's tool, we have to admit that we are broken. If a small group has subtle expectations that its members should have their lives "together," then members will be encouraged to keep their failings to themselves. Over time, individuals can begin to believe that this "corrected" version of themselves is in fact real. When this happens, it can become hard to see where we need God's transforming Spirit in our lives. Failings we will not admit cannot be transformed. It can also make it hard to welcome into the group others whose brokenness and struggles are obvious.

When a small group becomes focused on looking good for one another, the opportunities for real ministry become severely limited. Not only will this stand in the way of transformation for those individuals experiencing pain, it will also discourage honest sharing by members who have experienced failure and been transformed through it. In other words, when a group is formed on an expectation of looking good to one another, the broken are deprived of the good news God wants them to hear, and the transformed are deprived of the opportunity to share their story of transformation.

A healthy group creates a safe place for its members to talk honestly about their lives, without fear of whether the story is acceptable. The good news of God's acceptance is modeled through the lives of others who know that reality and can testify from their experience to the ever-present possibility of transformation. In a healthy group, the sharing of pain is not the focus of the group, either seeking it out or avoiding it. Instead, the good news that God is there with us through it all, loving us and reclaiming us, guides the honest sharing of the group. In a healthy group, the unpleasant parts of us are just as welcome as the pleasant parts, because being a disciple requires that we are real.

As a leader, pay attention to the sharing that happens in your group. Ask yourself these questions:

- Do people only share the positive stories from their lives or from their past?
- How does the group react when a story about a painful experience is shared?
- Is there a moral code that determines what is acceptable to talk about in the group?
- Are members forced to pretend about their lives or their past to fit into that moral code?
- Are others excluded or do they choose not to attend because they won't or can't pretend?

CHAPTER 6

Suggestions for Play and Team Building

Forming your group into a community will require trust. Trust is built over time, and in response to lots of different types of interaction. How someone is treated while doing dishes affects how willing they are to share in worship. Scheduling regular activities designed to form the group into a team will help grow the base of trust needed for the group to thrive.

Teams can either be cooperative or competitive. Competitive teams often thrive on "one-up-man-ship," or cutting humor that leads to the eventual pulling away of team members. Cooperative teams hold one another up. They look for good things to happen for one another. They are willing to risk without fear of ridicule. They have the potential to become a nurturing community. The kind of team your group becomes will be determined by the activities you choose. Here are some suggestions for activities you can do to help foster a trusting community.

- Devise an activity or relay that requires the entire group to accomplish a task. Have the group try it together, and have one person time it. Then work as a group to figure out how you can accomplish the same goal in less time.

- Give each person paper and colored pencils or markers. Have each participant divide their paper in four sections, and draw the four most important things in their life. Then have them find a partner they don't know well and explain to that partner what the drawings mean. The partner will then introduce them to the group using their drawing.

- Have one or more individuals prepare to share in a "spiritual show and tell." Have them bring something to show to the group that reflects what is spiritually significant for them.

- Write introductory questions about people's interests, or childhood, or occupation, and put them in a basket. Play a game that singles out one person, and when someone is singled out, have them draw a question and answer it for the group.

- Find a project the entire group can work on together. This provides a chance for those who are better with their hands to take on roles of leadership in the group.

- If you are a group that meets together weekly, consider a weekend trip or retreat together. Spending a few days together will create relationships that can't be formed in just a couple hours per week together.

- Schedule small group home visits with several members being hosted in another member's home. Being in someone's home deepens your relationship with that person.

If your group is open to physically active team-building exercises, there are many great books available for you. Tim Dodds, an experienced team builder and camping consultant, offers some of his favorites at the end of this section. To help you get started, Tim describes one of his favorite exercises for small groups: Wind in the Willows.

Wind in the Willows

This activity exists in countless team-building resources and is the tried and true standard of team building. *One word of caution, please be sure someone in your group is able to do some basic explanation of spotting techniques for safety. It is also important to communicate a "Challenge By Choice" policy that establishes that while everyone is encouraged to participate, no one will be asked or required to do something he or she is uncomfortable with. Honoring this always with gentle encouragement but no pressure is important. This too will add to the trust and community building your group experiences.*

Gather your group in a circle facing in. Participants need to stand shoulder to shoulder with hands held up, palms facing out, and elbows bent. This is called the "bumper position" and is the standard of **spotting positions**. Ask for one person to go first to stand in the center. The **center person** should cross their arms in front of them grabbing their right shoulder with their left hand and vice versa. Keeping their body stiff and knees straight, the center person will ask, "Spotters ready?"

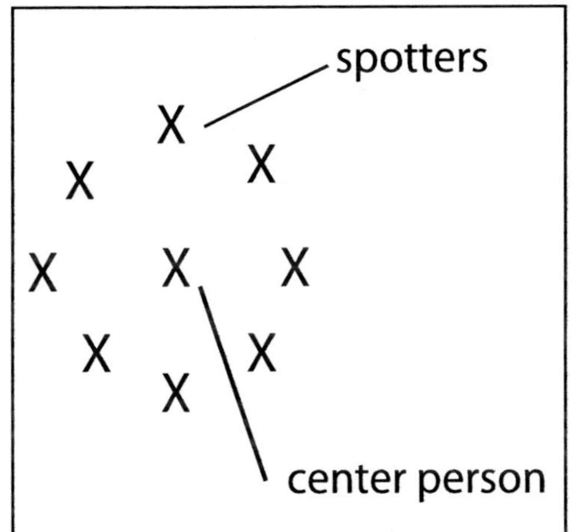

The spotters in the circle will look around the circle to determine if everyone is ready to proceed. If ready, they will say in unison, "Spotters are ready!" Center person then declares, "Falling" and spotters reply, "Fall away!" The center person then "falls" to the spotters who gently begin to move the center person around the circle. After a time or two around the circle, reverse directions. Finally, place the person back into the center of the circle. The experience is usually enhanced when the center person closes their eyes and the spotters are silent. Continue to invite group members to the center to take their turn.

When everyone who would like to participate has done so, debrief the activity with these kinds of questions:

- What was the experience like?
- Was it easy to trust others in the group?
- What was difficult?
- What was easy?
- How was this like life?
- What did you learn about yourself?
- What did you learn about others?

Team-Building Resources for Young Adults

Cowstails and Cobras II: A Guide to Games, Initiatives, Ropes Courses, and Adventure Curriculum, by Karl Rohnke
Kendall/Hunt Publishing Company ISBN 0-8403-5434-7 ©1989
4050 Westmark Drive, P.O. Box 1840 1-800-228-0810
Dubuque, IA 52004 *orders@kendallhunt.com*
  www.kendallhunt.com

***Funn Stuff Volume 1,* by Karl Rohnke**
Kendall/Hunt Publishing Company ISBN 0-7872-1633-X ©1996

***Funn Stuff Volume 2,* by Karl Rohnke**
Kendall/Hunt Publishing Company ISBN 0-7872-2316-6 ©1996

***Funn Stuff Volume 3,* by Karl Rohnke**
Kendall/Hunt Publishing Company ISBN 0-7872-4654-9 ©1998

***Funn Stuff Volume 4,* by Karl Rohnke**
Kendall/Hunt Publishing Company ISBN 0-7872-7133-0 ©2000

New Games Training CD-ROM
  Dale N. Le Fevre (770) 962-0514
  P.O. Box 1641 *dlefevre@can.org*
  Mendocino, CA 95460 *www.msn.org/a/newgames*

***Silver Bullets: A Guide to Initiative Problems, Adventure Games, and Trust Activities,* by Karl Rohnke**
Kendall/Hunt Publishing Company ISBN 0-8403-5682-X ©1984

***Teamwork and Teamplay,* by Jim Cain and Barry Jolliff**
Kendall/Hunt Publishing Company ISBN 0-7872-4532-1 ©1998

Quicksilver: Adventure Games, Initiative Problems, Trust Activities and a Guide to Effective Leadership, **by Karl Rohnke and Steve Butler**
Kendall/Hunt Publishing Company   ISBN 0-7872-2103-1   ©1995

Team-Building Resources for Young Adults and Children

Early Childhood Adventures in Peacemaking, **by William J. Kreidler and Sandy Tsubokawa Whittall**
Educators for Social Responsibility and Work/Family Directions   ©1999
23 Garden Street   (617) 492-1764
Cambridge, MA 02138   1-800-370-2515
educators@esrnational.org   *www.esrnational.org*

Adventures in Peacemaking: A Conflict Resolution Guide for School-Age Programs, **by William J. Kreidler and Lisa Furlong**
Educators for Social Responsibility and Work/Family Directions   ©1996

Family-Friendly Ideas Your Church Can Do
Group Publishing   ISBN 0-7644-2035-6   ©1998
PO Box 481   1-800-447-1070
Loveland, CO 80539   *info@grouppublishing.com*
                                          www.grouppublishing.com

Fifty-Two Fun Family Prayer Adventures: Creative Ways to Pray Together, **by Mike Nappa and Amy Nappa**
Augsburg Fortress   ISBN 0-8066-2841-3   ©1996
P.O. Box 1209   1-800-328-4648
Minneapolis, MN 55440-1209
customerservice@augsburgfortress.org
www.augsburgfortress.org

Parachute Games, **by Todd Strong and Dale LeFevre**
Human Kinetics   ISBN 0-8732-2793-X   ©1996
P.O. Box 5076   1-800-747-4457
Champaign, IL 61825-5076   *orders@hkusa.com*
                                          www.humankinetics.com

CHAPTER 7

Suggestions for Worship

Small group worship will grow out of, and be connected with, the other parts of your small group interaction. How you study and serve and play together will affect how you worship together. However, when you are pressed for time, it can be easier to default to a traditional worship format. When planning worship for young adults, the actual order of worship isn't nearly as important as the feel of the worship and the connections that are made. Here are a few suggestions:

Why Are We Worshiping?
Many have been to countless worship services without ever asking themselves why Christians worship together. Christians gather in worship to praise God, to be transformed, and to proclaim the good news that all are accepted, forgiven, and called to serve their Creator. As such, genuine worship will focus on God, not on the participants.

As you begin to plan a worship service, ask yourself what you want to emphasize.

> Are you wanting to raise an awareness of gratitude?
> Are you trying to challenge the participants to view their life in a
>   different way?
> Are you trying to create a quiet space to hear God's voice?

Once you have clear what you are seeking in worship, the elements should be aimed at guiding participants to that end. There are no rules that require certain elements in worship, such as a sermon, if it doesn't match the emphasis of the worship.

Make It Personal.
For most young adults, personal story and testimony are key elements to a meaningful worship. The good news isn't good news unless someone can tell them how it is changing their life today.

Don't Be Afraid to Use "Secular" Elements.
For many young adults, the difference between sacred and secular is not a significant distinction. They may find religious meaning in popular music or writing, as well as in religious music or writing. Don't be afraid to mix elements of both in worship. Encourage young adults to identify things they encounter that speak to them or challenge them and share those things in a worship setting. Movie clips, songs, articles, and paintings can all be significant parts of worship. While you need to be sure the worship affirms a sound theology, you don't need to be confined to "sacred" elements.

Use Applied Scripture.
Many young adults say they want to hear more scripture, but have it
applied to their lives rather than just read out loud. This may mean that
scripture readings are more like book reports, where the reading is
followed by a description of the circumstances surrounding the scripture
story, and a discussion of how young adults feel about the scripture and
its connection to their lives.

Participation Is Key.
In order to feel like participants in worship, rather than observers, young
adults need to be actively involved. Examples include circle prayers and
small group sharing. For some, a meaningful worship is created only
with the participation of everyone.

Music Is Important.
Music is an important part of worship. Music is often the only part of a
worship in which individuals participate together, and it can also serve
as a vehicle to affirm theology together. However, you cannot assume
that all young adults will prefer the same kind of worship music. Ask
the young adults in your group what type of music speaks to them. Ask
whether they prefer live or recorded music. Ask if they prefer a band, a
choir, a soloist, or instrumental music. The power of the music used will
depend on the involvement of the young adults in its selection.

Respect Diverse Worship Styles.
Different people find meaning in different styles of worship. This means
that not every worship element will be meaningful for every participant.
Work to foster an understanding among the young adults in your group
that some worships will be very meaningful for them, and others will be
less so but probably meaningful for others. Have diversity among your
worship planners to assure a wide variety of options. Also, you may
want to have a discussion about what speaks to each person in worship,
and be deliberate about identifying and trying to respect the differences
in worship styles within your group.

Silence Reflects Response.
For some who are more introverted, shy, hesitant, or new, the stillness
that comes in the midst of worshiping God is necessary for really
being able to "hear" or "feel" God's response. Whether as a time of
meditation, reflection, or a form of praise and prayer, silence or stillness
often provides the place where God's reality and our need for God sinks in.

CHAPTER 8

Suggestions for Scripture Study

How your group chooses to study is up to the group. The structure of the
time you spend studying should be a response to the needs, interests,
and abilities of your group members. For that reason, it is important
that when decisions are being made, everyone's opinion is heard and
valued. Below are several questions your group should discuss initially
and revisit as the needs and make-up of the group changes.

What Should We Study?

When you ask this question, you may find that the interests within your
group vary widely. You may also find that the list of topics the group
chooses could take several years to cover. When asked this question,
some young adults will list classes on life skills, such as budgeting,
car maintenance, or cooking. Others will respond with theological or
spiritual needs, like scripture study, prayer, or church history. So how do
you decide what to study and what to defer?

The first step is to return to your goals as a group. You are forming a
small group, not a university. The group simply cannot be all things to
all people. Ask the group to examine the list of suggested topics, and
consider these follow-up questions:

- Does this group have something unique to offer on this subject?
- Can I learn about this topic just as well or better from another
  source?
- Will learning about this topic with this group help me to be a
  better disciple?

Chances are, the answer to these questions will point toward a
combination of life skill classes and theological or spiritual classes. This
is healthy, and reflects the fact that learning to be a disciple involves
whole lives. In the Additional Resources section at the back of the book,
there are a few suggested texts that your group could use for study.

Who Should Teach?

Each group must decide whether to have an outside presenter or to
take turns having members of the group lead. Which approach your
group chooses will obviously depend on the topic, the skill level of the
members, and the availability of outside presenters. Some groups find a
real benefit in having members prepare to lead classes. It can encourage
leadership and gives those who lead a chance to delve more deeply into
the topic in preparation. Others find that an outside presenter can bring
a wealth of knowledge and experience not available among the young

adults. It can also provide an important chance to build bridges among the young adults and other members of the congregation. As is true with other questions, the group does not need to choose one approach exclusively and may change its approach over time.

How Long Should We Study One Topic?

Each topic will merit a different commitment of time. If you are just beginning, you may want to avoid making an extremely long commitment to one topic of study. The more your group matures, the more you will know about their primary areas of interest. Check back occasionally to make sure that the topic of study still matches the interest level of the group.

Differing Opinions

Your task as a leader is to help create a safe place for members of your group to honestly share their perspective. This is not an easy task and will require significant energy, thought, and prayer. Since young adults are in the process of defining their faith, your group will almost certainly have members with different views. It can be difficult to create a place where issues of importance are discussed, and participants are affirmed and challenged in their beliefs. One incident of heated debate can cause members to avoid all controversy, and consequently miss the learning that is possible in small group study.

Before your group begins dealing with potentially divisive issues, consider developing a group "contract" that describes how the group agrees to communicate. It is important for the group to develop this together since, to be effective, each person needs to agree to it. These basic ground rules for interaction should be placed where they are regularly visible as a reminder. You may find it helpful to refer back to the agreement on a regular basis, especially as new people join the group. Forming a community where it is safe to disagree takes time, and you may need to adapt the agreement as the needs of your group change.

While each group's agreement will look different, the facilitator of the process should be sure that the ground rules address topics such as the need for honesty, mutual respect of differing opinions, opportunity to be heard, confidentiality, and avoiding personal attacks. The leader of each session will be responsible for helping the group abide by the agreement and lovingly remind people when the agreement needs to be remembered. Below is a sample of what this type of agreement might look like:

Sample Group Covenant

- **All answers are acceptable.** There are no right or wrong answers. All participants are sharing a part of themselves as they respond to the question.
- **Demonstrate respect** for one another and one another's responses.
- **One person talks** at a time.
- **Listen with your whole self.**
- **Uphold confidentiality.** Things shared within the group are shared in trust. Be trustworthy with the things you learn about one another.
- **Offer and accept perspectives without attempting to persuade or convert.** When discussing emotional topics, try to use language such as, "I feel," or "for me."
- **Discuss the topic,** not other people's answers. Do not diminish or undermine the statements of others.
- **Be mindful of your choice of language;** choose words that are not offensive or divisive.*

Even with an agreement to treat one another with respect, disagreements will arise. While people are responsible for forming their own theology, this does not mean that any opinion someone chooses to hold is equally valid as any other. If any belief could pass as truth, there would be no point in seeking. Each person has a limited perspective, and no one can claim that they have a complete grasp of truth. Help the group create an atmosphere where each person's opinion is seen as a source to learn from. "While I may not agree with them, I can learn from understanding their perspective."

Different Styles

In any group, there will be members who look for chances to talk, and members who look for chances not to talk. No one should be forced to talk if they would rather be silent, but the depth of your study will be limited if only a few voices are heard. If you notice there are people who are not joining the discussion, look for ways to make space for them to share. Here are some steps to consider:

- Privately ask a member who is not sharing what would help make it more comfortable for them to speak.

*Adapted from Charmaine Chvala-Smith, *Called by a New Name: Group Guidelines for Listening Circles* (Independence, Missouri: Herald House, 2000), 52.

- After asking a question, take a moment for silent thought. Sometimes, those who require time to think are left behind by those who can answer immediately.
- Try going around the circle occasionally and giving each person a chance to talk or pass. Having an automatic turn without having to get the floor may make it more comfortable for quieter people to join the discussion.

If it becomes clear that only a few voices are dominating and others are unable to speak, you may need to seek loving ways for the group to manage its discussion time more equitably. Examples might be to set time limits for everyone or restrict the number of times a person can speak to a question. Another solution might be to have an object that determines who has the floor, so that it is clear whose turn it is to speak by who is holding the object. These ideas would need the approval of the group to be effective and should not be used to single anyone out. The goal is not to limit anyone's voice, but rather to make sure everyone's voice is heard.

Scripture Study[*]

The young adults in your group may choose to study scripture, but you may find that they have diverse feelings about scripture. These may include confusion, curiosity, reverence, or ambivalence. In spite of this, studying scripture as a small group can be a powerful activity. It is powerful because God uses the text of scripture to speak to people today. As you study, individual members may become aware of a personal calling in their life. However, without structure, a scripture study can become a debate over whose interpretation is correct, and the power of scripture will be missed. To reach beyond the surface meaning, scripture study must approach the text from three perspectives.

> **Looking at the text.** This is when you try to understand the words on the page. In this stage, you explore the who, what, when, where, and why of the text. For this stage, it is helpful to have a couple of introductory commentaries, such as that found in the New Oxford Annotated Bible. The leader, which may change from week to week, will prepare to make a short presentation (less than ten minutes) on the background of the text.

[*] These suggestions for scripture study are offered by Anthony and Charmaine Chvala-Smith who lead a weekly young adult scripture study in their home in Independence, Missouri. For more suggestions, see their articles in the May and July 2001 *Herald*.

Looking with the text. Place yourself in the scriptural story, and explore how that feels and looks. Where have you experienced similar things, or where do you have similar needs? This is where you stop questioning the text, and let the text question you.

Walking with the text. Ask yourself how the scripture may be asking you to change. How might this scripture affect how you see others? How can you practice these insights this week? This is where you apply the scripture to your actions.

It is easy for a scripture study to get stuck looking at the text and never move into the other perspectives. If this happens, you can find yourself mastering the information about the scripture, but never letting the scripture speak to you. In a group setting, this can lead to a single person delivering the "answers" in lecture form. This might answer questions of the head, but it will not answer questions of the soul. Doing all three stages of study will help the Word move beyond your head, through your heart, and into your will.

Below is a sample of how one young adult group does scripture study. This group has agreed that depth is more important that "finishing," and so they cover as little as one verse in a meeting and never more than one chapter. The group has agreed to three rules for how they will communicate:

1.   All answers are acceptable.
2.   Don't debate other's answers. Answer as if you were the first to answer.
3.   One person talks at a time.

The schedule used by this group could be adapted to the needs of your group, and could be lead by anyone who has read a couple of commentaries on the assigned text in advance. In this group, members take turns leading and no advance reading is required from the other participants.

Sample Scripture Study

7:00 p.m.	**Gather**
7:30 p.m.	**Opening Prayer and Sharing Good News**

Mixer: Question Jar (one person draws question from the previously created jar of questions, and every member must answer the question. The three rules listed on the previous page are applied.)

8:00 p.m. **Scripture Study**

Read scripture aloud. Go around the circle, each person reading a verse or two.

Example: "But when they saw [Jesus] walking on the sea, they thought it was a ghost and cried out; for they all saw him and were terrified. But immediately he spoke to them and said, 'Take heart, it is I; do not be afraid.' " Mark 6:49–50

Looking at the Scripture

- Ask what questions people have about the scripture.
- Compare different versions of the scripture.
- Look at footnotes in the text.

Looking with the Scripture

- Reread the scripture aloud.
- Ask questions about when people have experienced something like that in their own lives. Example, When have you been frightened by knowing that God was in your life?

Walking with the Scripture

- Ask a life application question. Example, Is there anyone in your life who needs to be reminded that Christ is there to calm the seas?

9:00 p.m. **Prayer Time**

9:30 p.m. **Food**

> **Suggestion**
> The Spiritual Formation Bible: New Revised Standard Version (Grand Rapids, Michigan: Zondervan, 1999) has questions similar to these in the margins of the text. It can serve as a starting point for leaders looking for discussion questions.

Tips for Scripture Study

- Try to keep people to the text, rather than using the scriptures as a springboard to their pet issues. When people fail to stick to the text, they often begin using the scriptures to tell others what they should do, rather than allowing the scriptures to speak to them. As leader, watch for those times when you need to gently bring the group back to the text.

- Be cautious about looking for parallels between the Gospels or between books of scripture. Allow the authors to speak for themselves, and try to hear what this author has to tell you.

- Be careful of study that becomes wrapped up in speculation. If the scriptures were a river, your study should be focused on the main channel, not the side channels of speculation. That main channel in the scriptures is the redeeming love of God made incarnate in Christ, and available to us through the Holy Spirit. When people become sidetracked in speculation, that message can be obscured.

- Not all scripture will apply to your context, and so it is okay to say "no" to a text. Theology and faith is informed by more than scripture alone. However, it can become easy to dismiss the things you disagree with, rather than allowing yourself to be challenged by them. You have to listen well before you can legitimately say "no." To avoid hiding from a scripture that challenges you, continually ask yourself, "What is this text calling me to in my discipleship?"

- The Word of God is a living thing, and when you let it into your life it will change you and your group in ways you cannot predict or control.

For leaders who want a more in-depth discussion of the approach to scripture, the following texts are recommended:

Luke Timothy Johnson, *Living Jesus: Learning the Heart of the Gospel* (San Francisco: HarperSanFrancisco, 1999). ISBN 0-0606-4283-1

M. Robert Mulholland, *Shaped By the Word: The Power of Scripture in Spiritual Formation* (Nashville, Tennessee: Upper Room, 2001). ISBN 0-8358-0936-6

CHAPTER 9

Suggestions for Service *

* These suggestions for service were offered by Todd Elkins, World Church minister at the Midlands Mission Center.

There are lots of reasons for a small group to be involved in serving together. Service helps form community. Service makes a difference in other people's lives. Service can bring in new members to the group. Service can energize the group by offering a hands-on project to work on. Planning for a service project helps grow leaders. But the most important reason for your group to be involved in service is because service is the natural response to belief. Faith is lived out in service to others. A small group that does not serve together will soon develop an inward focus.

> I was hungry and you gave me food, I was thirsty and you gave me something to drink, I was a stranger and you welcomed me, I was naked and you gave me clothing, I was sick and you took care of me, I was in prison and you visited me. Truly I tell you, just as you did it to one of the least of these who are members of my family, you did it to me.
>
> —Matthew 25:35–36, 40

Tips

- Begin by asking why you want to serve together. If a group is involved in service for reasons that only have to do with themselves, there is a good chance their service will only help themselves.

- Next, look at the needs around you. Look in your group, your congregation, and your community. What is not being done? Brainstorm a list of places you see need around you.

- Ask what gifts your group has to offer. Do you have people with construction abilities? musical talent? sewing abilities? free time? computer skills? listening ability? Make a list of the things your group could offer.

- Don't be afraid to partner with other organizations. Before you begin a Habitat for Humanity house of your own, work with an existing building project to help form the group's commitment. There are many terrific community organizations evaluating need and developing effective responses. While you shouldn't be shy about responding boldly if you feel called to offer something new, partnering with other organizations first can give you much needed information before you make large commitments of time and money.

- If your group is unsure about direction, try a variety of service projects to begin with. The first activity your group is involved in may not be a good match for the group. Serving in a variety of settings will help the group discern how it is called to serve.

- Look beyond the needs of your church. There are probably plenty of needs in your group or congregation that you could respond to. While that can help develop community and build bridges, don't exclude service projects outside your congregation. Part of the growth of service comes from interacting with people you may be conditioned not to see. Service can be life changing by exposing people to new understandings of those who are powerless.

- Schedule time to process your experience as a group afterward. In addition to helping the members reflect on the significance of the event for them, processing can also help the leaders decide if that project should be repeated or expanded. Some of the organizations you partner with may have an educational component to assist you with this step. Some questions to discuss during and after your service are:

> What did you learn?
> What made you uncomfortable?
> What surprised you?
> What moved you?
> What is the real need of the people you were serving?
> Why does this need exist?
> Who benefits from the existence of this need?
> How and why is our group involved?

- As the group begins to repeat projects, use the responses to these follow-up questions to approach the same problem from a different perspective. Rather than simply repeating the same project in response to the same need, consider asking each time how the group can plan a project that will get closer to the source of the problem.

- As your group matures, consider committing to a more involved, longer-term project. There is a depth of growth and understanding that comes only from struggling together to address a single need over time.

- Consider partnering with the larger congregation in some service projects. Working together can help build the type of trust that makes healthy intergenerational congregations.

- Some service projects are best done in a retreat setting. This allows the group to spend more time working together and to develop a familiarity with the task that might not be possible in just a Saturday morning project. Retreats also help form the group as a community.

- Service projects may attract a different group of people than other activities and may attract a smaller group. This is not a reason to avoid them. If the group is divided about whether or how to serve, try to agree to support one another even if it means only part of the group is involved. If you only do service projects everyone in the group wants, you may miss valuable opportunities to learn.

- Don't define service too narrowly. Not all service projects swing hammers. There are many organizations working to bring justice to unjust situations. Your participation in these projects might not be as hands on, but your impact on the underlying problem may be greater. For a couple of organizations experienced at helping small groups advocate for justice, check out Bread for the World at *www.bread.org*, or Amnesty International at *www.amnesty.org*. For more links, you can visit the Peace and Justice Ministries Web page at *www.CofChrist.org/peacejustice*.

- Use service opportunities to help grow leaders. Rather than relying on the existing leaders to make the plans, see if there is a new leader willing to organize the group's service project.

Other Resources on Service

Victor N. Claman, David E. Butler, and Jessica A. Boyatt, *Acting on Your Faith* (Boston: Insights, Inc., 1994). ISBN 0-9639-7010-0

Peter L. Benson and Eugene C. Roehlkepartain, *Beyond Leaf Raking: Learning to Serve/Serving to Learn* (Nashville, Tennessee: Abingdon Press, 1994). ISBN 0-6872-1328-2

Carl S. Dudley, *Basic Steps toward Community Ministry* (Bethesda, Maryland: Alban Institute, 1991). ISBN 1-5669-9048-3

CHAPTER 10

Suggestions for Retreat Planning

Another type of young adult group can be formed through regular young adult retreats. This is especially appropriate if distance prohibits your group from meeting more frequently. Here are some basic suggestions for planning a young adult retreat.

Planning

Planning a retreat can be an exercise of faith. Often retreat directors plan an entire retreat not knowing whether anyone will come. This can be discouraging, especially if you have never done it before. As much as you encourage pre-registrations, young adults are notorious for not registering in advance. The best way to assure that others will be in attendance is to involve them in the planning.

Having a leadership team also relieves anyone from having to be the sole leader. When a group leads together, greater community is formed. For this reason, try to make sure the retreat participants get a chance to work together, such as cooking or cleaning. As tempting as it may be to do it all yourself, everyone needs to feel needed. If there is no opportunity to work, some will go home feeling they weren't a part.

Publicity

As mentioned earlier, young adults often need to hear about an activity several times, in several different ways before they commit to participate. Begin putting the word out early, so people can plan ahead. Make a plan for how you are going to advertise the retreat, using several formats like e-mail, church bulletins, postcards, and personal phone calls. Retreats can also be advertised on the World Church Young Adult Ministries Web page.

Before you begin publicizing, be sure that you have approval on the idea and dates from the appropriate jurisdictional officer and the location reserved. Ask to have it placed on the jurisdictional calendar, as well as in any newsletter or announcements. A registration form should be available when you begin to publicize. Your publicity should include as much of the following information as possible:

    Date
    Location
    Theme
    Guest minister(s)
    Start time

End time
Cost
Contact person and contact information
Activities planned
Directions
What to bring
Emergency contact number at facility
Will there be programming for children?
Can people come for just the day or evening?

Location

Campgrounds can book quickly, so scheduling the date and booking the facility should be done early. If you do not have a church campground that is centrally located, think about using a retreat center or church building. While someone's home could be used, it is better to find a location where everyone is equally a guest, and where the group is really able to get away from the rest of the world.

Cost

The cost of the retreat will determine whether some people can attend. This is especially true if a married couple both want to attend. When scheduling the facility and activities, try to find ways to keep the cost at a minimum. You may want to ask a variety of young adults how much they would be willing or able to pay for a retreat, then try to plan the retreat for that cost.

You will want to prepare a budget for your retreat, and designate someone to handle the money. Talk with your bishop or stewardship commissioner about how the finances should be handled. Some jurisdictions have a budget for young adult ministry that may be available to assist if it is not possible for the retreat to be financially self sufficient.

Schedule

Young adult retreats are different from youth retreats. The schedule of a young adult retreat is usually more relaxed and tailored to the young adults in attendance. Starting later and staying up later seem to be common requests of young adults, but be sure to involve others in deciding the schedule. If you are offering children's programming, your schedule may need to be adjusted to accommodate families.

Young adult retreats are also different from youth retreats, because much of the supervision required with youth, such as counselors and lights out, are not appropriate with adults. This level of freedom may be difficult for younger young adults who might still be accustomed to youth activities. You may need to work as a group to develop a sense of responsibility, accountability, and trust on some of those issues.

Remember that the young adults who will attend are looking for something. The schedule should be structured to help them find what they came looking for. Make it clear that the activities are planned for them, but participation is by choice. Be sure to offer lots of free time for recreation, napping, private prayer, and socializing. While you certainly hope they will come to activities such as classes, they are adults, and they will decide for themselves which activities will best help them in their search.

When planning the start and end times, plan them to accommodate the travel and work schedules of those you know are coming. A sample schedule from both a young adult retreat and a young adult reunion can be found in the appendix.

Guest Ministry

If you decide to have a guest minister or ministers at your retreat, be sure that you invite ministers who relate well with young adults. They should understand that young adults are exploring, and be willing to listen as much as they talk. If they are presenting on a particular topic, they should have some expertise in that area. You may need to schedule some guest ministers more than a year in advance, and there may be an expectation that you pay at least their registration costs and possibly their travel expenses to attend. That should be clarified when you invite them.

If you decide you do not want to have a guest minister, you can use your class time as study time together. At the end of this book are several recommended study guides that could be lead by a young adult with some advance preparation. You could have each participant come ready to teach a class session from a common text, or on a topic they have expertise in. If you do not have a guest minister, try to make sure there will be someone in attendance who can act as a mentor for those who might need individual attention.

Other Staff

Some other staff may be required by your local campground policies or by state law. Find out if you are required to have a nurse on staff for the retreat. Also, be sure to ask whether you are required to bring your own cook. If you plan to do the cooking as a group, make sure that is allowed at the facility. If you are offering children's programming, make sure that everyone working with the children is a registered youth worker.

Additional Resources

This resource was intended as a basic introduction to forming a young adult group. For more in-depth reading on the subject, consider the following books:

Books on Small Groups

Jeffrey Arnold. *Starting Small Groups: Building Communities That Matter*. Abingdon Press, 1997.

Ken Baugh and Rich Hurst. *Getting Real: An Interactive Guide to Relational Ministry*. Navpress, 2000.

Deena Davis, compiler. *Discipleship Journal's 101 Best Small Group Ideas*. Navpress, 1996.

Terry Hershey. *Young Adult Ministry*. Group Publishing, 1986.

Thomas G. Kirkpatrick. *Small Groups in the Church: A Handbook for Creating Community*. Alban Institute, 1995.

Jimmy Long, editor. *Small Group Leaders' Handbook: The Next Generation*. Intervarsity Press, 1995.

John D. Schroeder. *How to Start and Sustain a Faith-Based Young Adult Group*. Abingdon Press, 2002.

Study Guides for Young Adults

Jeffrey Arnold. *Small Group Starter Kit: Six Studies for New Groups*. Intervarsity Press, 1995.

Gary L. Ball-Kilbourne. *Get Acquainted with Your Bible*. Abingdon Press, 1993.

Andrew Bolton. *Sermon on the Mount: Foundations for an International Peace Church*. Herald House, 1999.

Wayne Ham. *The Fourth "R" Religion*. (volumes 1–5). Herald House, 1995.

Richard K. Lindgren. *God on the Front Page*. Herald House, 2000.

Peace and Justice Ministries Team. *A Prophetic People Embrace Peace and Justice*. Herald House, 2001.

Power and Light for Adults. Herald House, periodic publication.

Several publishers offer a series of resources designed for small group study. They include:

- *20/30 Bible Study for Young Adults*, Abingdon Press. *www.cokesbury.org*

- *Intersections*, Augsburg/Fortress Publishers. *www.augsburgfortress.org*

- *Lifesearch*, Abingdon Press. *www.cokesbury.org*

Books about Young Adults

Tom Beaudoin. *Virtual Faith*. Jossey-Bass, 1998.

Robert T. Gribbon. *Developing Faith in Young Adults*. Alban Institute, 1990.

Craig Kennet Miller. *Postmoderns*. Discipleship Resources, 1996.

What Next? Connecting Your Ministry with the Generation Formerly Known as X. Augsburg Fortress, 1999.

Contact Information for Support

For assistance or ideas in young adult ministry, contact

Young Adult Ministries
1001 W. Walnut
Independence, MO 64050-3562

1-800-825-2806, ext. 1363
youngadults@CofChrist.org

For information on finding young adult ministers near you or for information about young adult retreats and reunions, visit the Young Adult Web page.

www.CofChrist.org/yadults

Closing Thoughts

There is an overwhelming amount of need among young adults, and so the call to respond can seem overwhelming as well. While I hope that these lessons learned by other young adult ministers will help you start in the right direction, they will not eliminate the struggles ahead. Struggle is a natural and necessary part of serving. When the struggles surface, remember that real ministry does not come from you; it comes through you. Nothing can equal the joy of being used as a tool by God. When you give yourself in service to God, accepting whatever happens, only one outcome is certain: you will be changed.

Appendix: Sample Schedules

Sample Weekly Meeting

5:00   Gather to make dinner.
5:30   Form a circle and have each person share a good thing or a bad thing from their week, then pray over the meal.
5:45   Eat dinner together.
6:15   Do dishes.
6:30   Class or games.
7:30   End with a circle prayer.

Sample Young Adult Retreat Schedule
Theme: Spiritual Renewal

Friday

7:00   First meeting: introductions and mixers
8:30   Campfire
9:15   Games

Saturday

8:30   Breakfast
9:15   Spiritual renewal session
10:15   Break
10:45   Spiritual renewal session
Noon   Lunch and nap
2:00   Free time
              (options: mountain biking, hiking, personal prayer, games)
6:00   Supper
7:00   Spiritual renewal session
8:30   Campfire
9:15   Games

Sunday

8:30   Breakfast
9:15   Meditative walk
10:00   Communion service
11:00   Check out; break camp

Sample Young Adult Reunion Schedule
Theme: Discovering the Divine in the Ordinary

Sunday

3:00–6:00 p.m.	Registration
6:00	Dinner
7:30	Welcome, group activities
9:30	Campfire

Monday, Tuesday, Wednesday, and Friday

8:30	Breakfast and clean up
9:30	Worship
10:15	Class
Noon	Lunch and clean up
1:30	Activity (followed by free time)
6:00	Supper and clean up
7:00	Group activity/discussion
9:30	Campfire
10:30–?	Games, fellowship

Thursday

8:30	Breakfast, clean up and make lunches
9:30	Worship
10:15	Leave for beach
8:30	Return, clean up
9:30	Campfire
10:30–?	Games, fellowship

Saturday

8:30	Breakfast and clean up
9:00	Pack and camp clean up
10:00	Closing worship
11:30	Break camp

Class Schedule

Monday	Spiritual Growth
Tuesday	Young Adult Ministry: Group Discussion
Wednesday	Stewardship
Thursday	Beach trip
Friday	Life Balance

Afternoon Activities

Monday	Ropes course
Tuesday	Rock climbing
Wednesday	Canoeing
Thursday	Beach trip
Friday	Free day (golf, mountain biking, shopping)

Evening Activities

Monday	Town trip
Tuesday	Group discussion
Wednesday	Worship
Thursday	Beach trip
Friday	Group discussion

Success Stories

Photo: George Williams

Flagstaff, Arizona: This Young Adult Group meets once a month on Sunday at 11:30 a.m. Meetings include food, worship, and recreation. Because the local congregation does not own a building, the group meets in the home of the leader. In the three years they have been meeting, they have gathered for barbeques, ordinations, hikes, picnics, pancake brunches, ring-toss tournaments, and a "snow frolic." Periodically, the young adults plan the worship for the local congregation.

Photo: Jessica Garvin

Central Michigan University in Mt. Pleasant, Michigan: Young adults in Michigan, meet in the student activity center for meals and recreation twice a week. The group, which is led by students, occasionally helps plan worships for the local congregation.

Photo: Leah Christensen

Greater Vancouver branch, British Columbia, Canada: "The Network" scripture study meets weekly after church at the Greater Vancouver branch, British Columbia, Canada. In addition to their weekly study, the group has expanded to include social gatherings and service projects. Leaders make a conscious effort to plan activities that will assist young adults with specific discipleship skills using the model of the path of the disciple.

Seattle, Washington: Young adults meet twice a month in homes. Activities rotate among service projects, book and movie reviews, fellowship, and worship. The group also holds retreats periodically at the church-owned campground. They have been meeting for four years.

Chicago, Illinois: "Youthful Christian Adults" have been meeting for five years. They meet in local congregations three times per month, and they gather at the local campgrounds three times per year. They have a leadership council that meets annually for a planning retreat and quarterly for follow-up meetings.

Denver, Colorado: "Circle of Friends" meets weekly for food and fellowship. Following the meeting, those who wish can stay for band practice. Membership in the band is open to anyone, and the band travels extensively playing for congregations throughout Colorado and beyond. The group has been meeting in homes since March 1999.

Grand Rapids, Michigan: Young adults and young families meet every other Monday at the church for a scripture study. The group also plans a fellowship activity once per quarter and occasionally plans the Sunday morning worship, inviting young adults from surrounding areas.

Independence, Missouri: Young adults and community volunteers worked together to build a playground at the Stone Church during the Young Adult Temple Event held in June 2000. The playground was based on ideas submitted by neighborhood children and was constructed in only four days.

Iowa City, Iowa: Young adults meet weekly for games, visiting, eating, and other activities. They alternate between meeting in the church or meeting in homes. Because many of the young adults are college students, the group varies greatly from year to year.

Notes